THOMAS LÉLU

TODAY IS A GOOD DAY TO ...

LEDUC

Conseil éditorial : Ariane Geffard
Édition : Marie Piquet
Maquette et design de couverture : Johanna Fritz
Photographie de couverture : © Thomas Lavelle

76 boulevard Pasteur
75015 Paris — France
ISBN : 979-10-285-3484-4

Ce carnet appartient à :

....

I NEED

TO

FORGIVE :

I AM :

WHO IS
YOUR
HERO?

I WANT
MORE:

I WANT
LESS :

WHAT
IS YOUR
NICKNAME?

WHY?

WHAT
TIME IS
IT?

WHERE
ARE
YOU GOING
THIS
EVENING?

WHAT IS A GOOD QUESTION?

ME + YOU

=

PEOPLE ARE:

WOULD YOU
LIKE YOU
IF YOU MET
YOU?

WANT SOME COFFEE?

TOMORROW will BE :

GIVE YOUR
LIFE
A RATING:

/10

MY MENTAL
STATE IS:

TODAY
IS A GOOD
DAY TO
...

ME :

LIFE :

THINGS YOU MIGHT NEED TO HEAR TODAY:

1)

2)

THINGS
TO DELETE:

1)

2)

3)

A WORD
TO REPLACE
NO :

I WAS
STRONG
LAST YEAR
THIS YEAR
I will BE:

GOOD
THINGS
HAPPEN
WHEN YOU :

OR WHEN :

I SPEND
50% OF MY
LIFE
LOOKING FOR:

WHAT
I'M
MISSING AT
THE
MOMENT IS:

THE FUTURE

will BE:

GIVE ME COFFEE FOR :

I DON'T THINK THAT:

I TOLD
MY THERAPIST
THAT :

I WOULD
LIKE YOU
TO BE:

AND:

TO DO list :

1)

2)

3)

DON'T
SPEND
ANOTHER
YEAR
DOING :

TODAY
OR NOT
TODAY

ALTERNATIVE
RESPONSES
TO I LOVE
YOU :

1)

2)

3)

MY
GUILTIEST
PLEASURE :

I ...

YOU

VERY MUCH

A WISE
DOCTOR
ONCE WROTE:

EVERY
JOURNEY
BEGINS
WITH :

WHEN
I WAS
LITTLE
THE FUTURE
WAS :

THE
SECRET
OF HAPPINESS
is :

SOME
PEOPLE ARE
WISE
AND SOME
ARE :

HOW TO STOP TIME?

TALENTLESS

BUT :

I'M IN MY

...

ERA

WE'RE
GOING TO
NEED
A lOT OF :

EXPECT :

APPRECIATE :

plans :

moves :

life :

prayers :

MOOD :

THREE WISHES:

1)

2)

3)

A SUNDAY MORNING:

1)

2)

3)

WHAT

A

...

DAY

WE WANT :

THE COOLEST PEOPLE I KNOW :

1)

2)

3)

INTELLIGENCE is :

I NEED :

NAME
SOMETHING
THAT YOU
COULD EAT
EVERY DAY:

IT'S OK

TO :

IT'S
NOT NECESSARY
TO :

I HATE :

1)

2)

3)

THREE RULES
TO REMEMBER
IN LIFE:

1)

2)

3)

HOW TO
BE IN
THE MOMENT?

1)

2)

3)

I WANT

TO :

1)

2)

MAKE :

NOT :

I USED
TO BE:

BUT I AM:

REMEMBER :

YOUR
FAVORITE
CHILDHOOD
MEMORY :

RESPECT
PEOPLE WHO:

I WOULD
NEVER
WANT
TO BE :

TODAY
I DID :

THINGS NO ONE SHOULD SAY DURING SEX:

1)

2)

3)

THREE
important
Guidelines
in Life:

I look
BETTER
WHEN I :

GO
HOME
AND
MAKE :

WHO DO
YOU TRUST:

WHAT DO
YOU NEED
RIGHT
NOW ?

LET'S :

THE only
THiNGS I
liKE
MORE THAN
READiNG
BooKS iS:

I DREAM
OF :

IT'S OK IF:

HOW WAS
YOUR DAY?

WHAT'S
THE SCARIEST
THING I
COULD BE
FOR HALLOWEEN?

TODAY
I DECIDED
THAT I AM :

LIFE TIPS:

1)

2)

WHO
IS YOUR
FAVORITE
ARTIST
LIVING OR
DEAD ?

MY FAVORITE
SEASON IS :

THE
OPPOSITE
OF A
FEMINIST
IS :

MY SEX
LIFE
IS LIKE:

TOP THREE
BANDS:

1)

2)

3)

YOU loose
MORE
BY :

THAN :

HOW TO
FIX
SOMEONE:

WHAT'S
ON YOUR
MIND RIGHT
NOW?

PERKS OF BEING AN ARTIST:

1)

2)

3)

THE BEST
3 DOCTORS:

1)

2)

3)

I'M PROUD
OF :

SORRY
WE'RE.

I'M
REALLY
GRATEFUL
FOR :

THE PURPOSE
OF LIFE
IS TO:

I DON'T
SAY IT
ENOUGH
BUT :

PROTECT YOUR :

I WAS
CREATED
TO :

FEELING
EXCITED
AND :

MAKE
MORE :

Cet ouvrage est composé de matériaux issus de forêts
bien gérées certifiées FSC®, de matériaux recyclés
et de matériaux issus d'autres sources contrôlées.

FSC
www.fsc.org
MIXTE
Papier | Pour une gestion forestière responsable
FSC® C007507

Achevé d'imprimer en septembre 2025 par Graphycems
Dépôt légal : octobre 2025
Imprimé en Espagne